He drew a circle that shut me out—
Heretic, rebel, a thing to flout.
But love and I had the wit to win:
We drew a circle that took him in.
Edwin Markham

Our task must be to free ourselves by widening our circle of compassion
to embrace all living creatures and the whole of nature and its beauty.
Albert Einstein

Until he extends his circle of compassion to include all living things,
man will not himself find peace."
Albert Schweitzer

Let architects sing of aesthetics that bring Rich clients in hordes to their
knees; Just give me a home, in a great circle dome Where stresses and
strains are at ease.
R. Buckminster Fuller

Create around one at least a small circle where matters are arranged as
one wants them to be.
Anna Freud

A circle is the reflection of eternity. It has no beginning and it has no
end - and if you put several circles over each other, then you get a spiral.
Maynard J. Keenan

The work itself has a complete circle of meaning and counterpoint. And
without your involvement as a viewer, there is no story.
Anish Kapoor

The bureaucracy is a circle from which one cannot escape. Its hierarchy is a hierarchy of knowledge. The top entrusts the understanding of detail to the lower levels, whilst the lower levels credit the top with understanding of the general, and so all are mutually deceived.
Karl Marx

And I say the sacred hoop of my people was one of the many hoops that made one circle, wide as daylight and as starlight, and in the center grew one mighty flowering tree to shelter all the children of one mother and one father.
Black Elk

"Never, never rest contented with any circle of ideas, but always be certain that a wider one is still possible."
Pearl Bailey

"It is very easy to think productively once we understand the mandala, and the circular movement, because we can always choose which side of a pair to see."
Carl Jung

We have created many different names for the same idea: circle, gravity, Abraxas, Aghuramazda, Allah, Aten, Bog, Brahma, Buddha, Christ, Elohim, Eru, God, Jesus, Jumala, Kami, Krishna, One, Shang Ti, Shiva, Trimurti, Vishnu, Waheguru, Yahweh, Yhwh. The circle, finally, clarifies, unifies, integrates and simplifies the ideas and symbols in science, psychology, philosophy, and religion. Our multiple names can confuse us and keep us away from our own 'truth.' It's, really, all in the circle, and everything's a circle. The circle, itself, is Absolute Intelligence.
Ilexa Yardley

Eco Leadership
The Power of the Circle
by David Aubrey Berger

Living University Press. Toronto

Enjoy these ideas, share them, try them out and be kind… support our work and vision. Invite Eco Leadership and a Living Education into your life and the lives of those you touch. Order more books! Thanks, we appreciate you.

Berger, David Aubrey
Eco Leadership: The Power of the Circle
ISBN 978-0-9730958-2-1

Concept, Design, graphic design, and layout: Darinka Blagaj
Editing: Darinka Blagaj, Copy Editing: Honey Thomas
Cover design by Darinka Blagaj
Cover photo by Darinka Blagaj and David Berger
Technical & Layout: Ed Ng, Tech. assistant: Shelly Sarkar

First Printing, August 2002
Second Printing, November 2002
Third Printing, October 2006
Fourth Printing January 2009

The Living University Press

www.LivingUniversity.com
dberger@LivingUniversity.com

Dedication

For the great mother from
which we all come, and to
which we all return.
Teacher, guide, companion.
May we, your children honour
ourselves, and each other on
our earth journey.

To the spirits of the four directions:
the east from where comes the light,
the south from where comes trust,
the west from where comes darkness,
and the north from where comes wisdom.

And to the path that we each
follow. May it be full, and
flowing with life in all its
manifestations.

Thank You

To Darinka,
my life love, wife, partner and friend.
Her light guides what follows to shine.

To my mother, Gloria,
who has been present in ways
I cannot imagine.

To my grandmothers
who have only recently passed on.

To my father, Michael,
for his love and encouragement
for me to always be me.

And to the special lights in my life:
Tamalei
&
Saskia

~: d.a.b :~

Life is change...
Growth is optional...
Choose wisely...

~: Karen Kaiser Clark :~

At every moment you must be
prepared to give up all that you
have for all that you want.

Contents

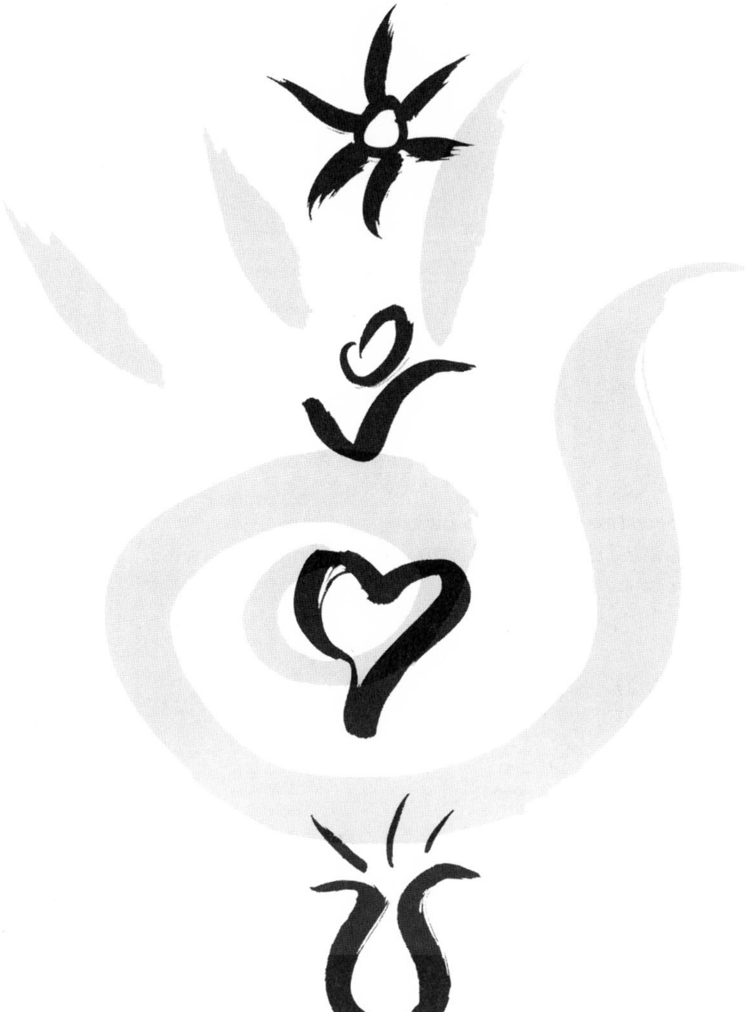

The experience of the self is
always a defeat for the ego.

Carl Jung

From the Author

It has been four years since I completed this book. Much has changed, and yet in some ways nothing has changed. My perspective on what this book is about has deepened. I set out to inform the teachers and the facilitators, the educators and those that design our learning structures. This new edition is for the leaders, the learners and the educators. We all carry the learnings, the openings and the closings, that come by spending time within the educational systems of our youth–reflection upon it offers insight and new ways of moving forward.

In this edition, I set out to offer inspiration and practices to all those who lead-in our families, institutions, and businesses. By changing ourselves we alter our culture. Some of you are teachers and facilitators, all of us are leaders in our shared journey together on planet earth. I aim these thoughts at a culture ready, wondering, and striving to be more in tune with the natural world. Eventually the trees will notice!

The roots of this book stretch back to when I was teaching first and second year students at York University I realized that their questions were larger than the subject I had been hired to teach. I felt like the job I was hired to do limited their experience of reality. I was supposed to act as if the information I had learned over the years was also important to them. I soon realized that they were not in my class to merely learn information. They were there to take the next step in life.

Living Education^tm is a facilitation style that brings together life and learning–resulting in way of leading that honours the earth–Eco Leadership.

If you are a leader, who does not spend time in classes consider my mentioning of classes akin to experiences, and leadership opportunities; the students are those you lead, and the curriculum is whatever systems you sustain or help create.

I hope and trust, that the ideas and thoughts in this book will assist in your positive growth, in your happiness, and in our collective ability to enjoy life on earth together.

David Aubrey Berger
Toronto, December 17th, 2008

A Way to Begin

I awoke pre-sunrise, slipped out of my sleeping bag, out of my hammock, into my shoes and shorts. I paddled into thick mist, so thick that I couldn't tell if it was a cloudy day or if it would burn off with the sun. I stopped close to the reeds at the end of the lake. I got out my recorder and played to the mist, to the trees, and to whatever else was listening. After a while a loon called back. The loon came close in the mist to hear this new strange bird out on the lake. I could see it surface close by, I heard the loon's call mix in with my sound, and I played on, knowing that I was as much a part of the scene as the mist, sun, water, loon. To me that is what music, and life, is all about: being at one.

There is a Hopi prophesy carved into the stone near Third Mesa in Arizona—the oldest continually inhabited town in the Americas. The prophecy says that at some point a white brother will return and bring a cross. Originally, the cross was contained within a circle, if he brings back only the cross, be careful, he has forgotten the interconnectedness of all things. From then, the world will move along in two ways, the first, the way of nature, or the Hopi way, and the other, the way of technology. At some point there comes an

opportunity to reconnect the way of technology to the way of nature or, the prophecy says, to head off to destruction.

This is that time. The time to reconnect the way of technology with the way of nature, the way of the sacred with the way of rational knowledge, product with process, information with inspiration, learning with life.

It is not what you do, but how you do it. It is not who you are, but how you are. My leading wandered out of the wilderness, as a camp counsellor leading and playing with kids for a summer, to guiding youth, and then adults on canoe trips. Into a classroom at York University, teaching environmental studies, and out of the classroom to lead drumming and drum-making workshops. Then back to the woods to run an annual summer solstice retreat festival of art and healing, and now to facilitate leadership and facilitation workshops.

All along I have held onto the belief that each person I meet is on a sacred journey to places I cannot imagine. All they need is the awareness that the journey is their own. Some inspiration, information and experience can help.

Imagine that everyone in the world is
enlightened–Except you.
And they are doing exactly
what they have to
in order to help you
achieve enlightenment.

–The Buddha–

The Way In

The value in the words that follow
lies more in your ability to be present
than in any wisdom I may offer.
The more present you are,
the more able you are to change,
to grow, to be free.

Accept all you are today, here and now.
You are the source of all of your strength.
Keep whatever set of beliefs you come with.
Add to them what you find useful here.

Consider this a process
a temple to walk into,
a hike through the woods, a prayer.
Not a map or a prayer book.

To enter requires your presence.
The subject is you.

Take several breaths now!
As deeply and slowly
as you are able.

Living Education

In these next few pages, I want to take you on a journey...

...an exploration of my own educational journey, and how it has influenced my ideas about learning. In the process, at the same time, I ask that you, take the opportunity to reflect on your own educational process. Find what relates to you, think up new thoughts about your perspective on learning. Consider what you gained and lost in the process. How it helped create you, and how it got in the way of you becoming yourself.

What do you remember from kindergarten, grade three, high school, university, college? Was it the people, history class, geography, math, Shakespeare, how to read and write? A teacher who inspired you, or one you disliked? A good friend, a group of friends, a team you played on? It is probably still the same today, children and teenagers getting through the system. Where are they going? Who do they get to be now? How can they know themselves today and envision a future from that? What is the best way to help them?

From the preliterate world of childhood we create our literate society. On September 2nd, 1970, at 9:00 a.m., along with millions of other Canadian children, I began grade 1. I was six years old. I had already learned a great deal; I could talk, walk, think, play, eat, dress myself. And to my own credit, and that of the other children with whom I began school, I had learned all of this from watching, listening and copying those around me. None of this was in the school's curriculum; we were expected to arrive with these skills.

Why did I go to school? Well, I didn't have any other choice. All of the other children were there, my father was at work, our nanny was busy keeping house, and my four-year-old brother was in nursery school.

I remember eating paste in kindergarten. At lunch break in primary school, I ran home to eat and watch the Flintstones. In grade five our class took a trip to Quebec City; in grade six we went to the Boyne River Outdoor Education Centre, and camped out in minus thirty-degree weather. In grade seven English class, the Vice Principal came in to teach us grammar because our teacher, Mrs. Friedman, said she did not know it. I remember Mr. Mitchell, our grade eight homeroom teacher, who ate lunch by himself in his car, listening to the BBC news. He often sent students to the back of the class or out into the hall for talking. And most fondly, from grade eight, I remember Mr. Walton, the shop teacher, with whom I often ate lunch, and with whose help I built a canoe.

In school, I got used to learning things. And I began to believe that those things would later be useful. In the process I must have stopped my own assessment of what I wanted to learn for myself. I learned: letters, printing, reading, numbers, addition, geography, multiplication, calculus, physics, history, music, French and more. I did not know what I would need it for. Some things were great, but most of what I learned did not have a 'later'. It got lost along the way.

Five percent of what university students learn they retain three years after graduation. What are we really doing at school anyway, and why has it become so important? Why do our children spend the best part of each day there?

Education:
Complex, Lifelong & Unplanned

In medieval society, all education was complex, lifelong and unplanned. Today it is the result of conscious design by teachers, boards of education, government policy-makers, parents and others—but not usually by the children, youth, and teenagers who attend school.

With the advent of the printing press in 1436, it became possible to educate a large group of people, in diverse settings, with the same ideas. This was the real beginning of mass education. And from Gutenberg's press onwards, schoolbooks have been the printing press' main business. They allowed, and encouraged, the development of the 'expert.' Down this road, family tradition, local custom, and personal preferences become second to any efficiency and 'the standard' or the 'norm'. The teacher, the classroom and the textbook became excellent tools of progress and efficiency. The rise and speed of the popularity of schools is amazing. For example, we find that in Bohemia in 1775 there were an estimated 30,000 children in school (15-16%). By 1779 that number had doubled, by 1784 it had reached 119,000 (59%), and by 1828, 91% of the children frequented primary school (Chartier 213).

Schools tend to obscure the simple fact that the only real source of knowledge is nature. Curriculum is too often designed as an end in itself—the student becomes secondary. Today's conscious design is tomorrow's hurdle. Schools, teachers, textbooks educate with one over-arching problem: all things change. Society, knowledge, people.

Getting Through It

In the present educational setting, students 'get through' school with the belief that they will be ready to enter the work world after

their education is complete. On average, people change careers every five years. Students take jobs to get them through school. A holding tank where we spend the first quarter of life to get ready for the modern world?

With the degree of specialization in our society, it actually takes people longer to grow up. In the 40's it was common for people to go to work at the age of fourteen, a century ago this age was eight or nine. We are capable of being responsible people in the world much sooner than we are offered the opportunity. Which is not to say we should be put to work at a younger age, but recognize that ability may develop at any age.

Our first sense of the world is that all things are connected. We naturally care about everything, most importantly our own freedom and well being. When we do not act on our instinct in the moment, we are deferring the taking of responsibility for our larger self (including the natural world, other cultures, etc.). This passivity is taught to children, accepted by youth (not always calmly), and often becomes habit for adults.

When my son was four years old, he came to me complaining that he did not know what to do. I said, "Great! When I do not know what to do, I sit and meditate—just breathe until an idea comes to me." This is perhaps one of the most important lessons anyone can learn. In our society of quick movement, where we accept the saying 'don't just sit there, do something,' the more profound lesson of 'don't just do something, sit there' is lost. And without the art of reflection we are confined to doing either what others are doing around us, the first thing that comes to mind, or what is expected. And the true source of innovation, inspiration and creativity is inaccessible. . . ourselves.

Connected & Disconnected Knowledge

Going down the road of information for the sake of information, risks separating an individual from their experienced world. When learning is driven by desire, it helps develop individuals who know what they want and why. When theory drives education, and concepts are taught that it will be useful 'sometime', we require the young to trust our judgement of what they will need rather than letting them figure it out for themselves. This develops individuals who are separate from what they want, more likely influenced by what there is, and who may not consider thoughts about what there could be. The result is a society of people who do not trust themselves or each other.

Connected and disconnected knowledge can be the same information—but set in different contexts. Connected knowledge is sought for a purpose that you want or need. Disconnected knowledge—learning the alphabet or algebra, without understanding its purpose—separates you from your desire to accomplish something in the world. It encourages a predisposition towards the future. As we wait to discover the purpose of what we are learning, we disregard the present. This seems to help individuals accept crowding, bad air and bad water.

The real questions are simple: Who are you? What do you want to do? How do you want to serve the greater whole? And yet they are so quickly obscured, to the point where they become inaccessible from deep within.

Not the Engines of Society

Schools bring together people of similar ages, in a setting separate from the everyday world of people creating, making things, and helping each other to live and make a living. Schools are their own reality. They become a large part of the people's lives who teach and run them, and of course, the central reality of children's lives (up to about the age of twenty-two).

They are not, however, the engines of society. But, once they are created, and students arrive, schools become alive for those who are present. In order to be interesting and relevant for the students, they have to be connected to their present reality.

As educators acknowledge that changing times will affect what their students need, the students will recognize the system is a helpful part of their lives. Until then, it's a Catch-22 game of, 'If you don't like me, I won't like you.' The board's curriculum, the teacher's lesson plan versus the student's desire. And the winner? No one. The loser? Society.

How do we address these issues with the high numbers of students and the limited budgets for paying teachers and creating curriculum? To start, some time must be allowed for the students themselves to recognize why they are there, and what they want to get from the class. They do not have to tell the teacher—they can tell each other. Doing this allows them to acknowledge their opinions, thoughts and feelings; they can become real, and present. Each one of us likes to be acknowledged for who we are, and when we are welcomed, we relax and are ready to learn. From this point, a living education begins.

Desire: The True Gift of Learning

I did not know what I wanted to do after high school. So, I took a year 'off'. I worked and traveled. It set me aside from my peers who ventured off to the campus and the pub together. I started on a kibbutz in Israel, and then made my way through Greece and Western Europe. I went to the running of the bulls in Pamplona, Spain, a music festival in Denmark, stayed in an old farmhouse in the Swiss countryside, and visited Amsterdam.

In Amsterdam I stayed in one of the many hostels in that town. Eating breakfast one morning, I started talking to an older fellow traveler from Germany. He said he wished he had gone to university, wished he had taken the time for the exploration and the growth. Hearing this was refreshing; most of the people I knew complained about school, and boasted about the extra-curricular activities. From that moment on, I started looking forward and found a developing appreciation for something that I had previously felt expected to do, confused by and uninterested in.

I was already planning to go to university. Deep down I knew that there was much I wanted to learn. But I had never linked my learning in a school with my life. The two were separate. Somehow school was in the 'learn to make money' category where I was supposed to get my training to be 'a something.'

Learning and the Land... Time...

I was not a good high school student. I just was not motivated to be present. I did not know what, or who, my learning was for. When I did finally arrive at university I wanted to be there. For the first time in my life I got A's and B's. For my second year I applied to, and got into, a one-year overseas programme in Jerusalem. I loved it. The year started with a six week Hebrew language class. I felt as if learning the language was an introduction to the land, and its people.

Along with studying Hebrew I studied, psychology, geography, political science and mysticism. Most memorably, I hiked. There was a hiking club at the university; almost every weekend a group of us would get on a bus to travel to one or another end of the country and hike through river valleys, across deserts, and over mountains. I put my head into the rivers and drank; I picked fruit off the trees. I felt as if I was busy connecting the information I learned through the week to the land that surrounded me. And all through the land were stories of what had happened there. Sodom and Gomorrah in the Judean hills, Jesus walking on the Sea of Galilee in the north. A land filled with story, in a way that made it alive, I had never experienced this before.

In North America, old age for a building is a around a century, with the exceptions around two hundred years. In the Middle East people pull out bibles and point to a site and quote what happened there two or three thousand years ago, as if it were yesterday. Walls five or six hundred years old surrounded me. Looking down from the fortress of Masada, where the Jews hid after the destruction of the second temple, you can see the outline of the Roman walls in which the soldiers camped. And you can walk up the ramp that they built to get to the top.

A half-day's walk from Jerusalem through the 'wadi', or river valley, lies the town of Jerico and the layers of the ruins of the older Jerico dating back over seven thousand years. I came home knowing that learning can be linked to a place, and that human society stretches out through time.

Out of the Middle Ages

The university system came out of the church schools of the Middle Ages. At Sorbonne in Paris, in 1271, a group of the monks studying there realized that they were doing something more than running a theological faculty to train the clergy. They became a faculty of philosophy and arts by asking the king and the Pope to grant them a unique position as a university. Their new status recognized the depth, and specialization to which they were exploring the subject—God. Even into this century, North American universities had roots in the churches. But that has mostly changed. Now their mandate is research, education, and publication.

Our educational style is also built on older foundations—the rhetorical, philosophical beliefs of Socrates. He tells us that the only true way to know something is to set the body and emotions aside and let the mind, with its reason, determine its true nature. To this day, thought, reason, rhetoric remain pillars in our educational systems. Greek thought was first challenged by Galileo in the 16th century, when he used experiments to disprove many of Aristotle's assumptions.

Today the frontier for education is individual experience, as the popularity of experiential education, action research, and individual learning styles show. I believe the frontier of tomorrow's education is emotion and spirit. The spiritual component of information is the way in which it connects to the whole of life. The emotional component is how it affects people's emotional world. This type of education will happen as educators learn to recognize the emotional and spiritual components of the material that they are teaching.

I graduated from university with a B.A. in philosophy, and went on to study at McGill in Montreal for a year. I felt as if I had entered an Ivory Tower, one professor had us read chapters of his upcoming book that explained how everything that happens is predetermined. I enjoyed my time in Montreal because of the McGill folk society—a group of students who met Tuesday nights to sing songs together. Somewhere I saw a poster for the Faculty of Environmental studies at York University, and I applied.

Sharing a Planet

At the faculty of environmental studies I finally felt as if I had arrived home. It was the first time I had met people who recognized the connection of nature to society—who knew deep down like I do—that without the wildness, the air, water and the hundred trillion or more ants who share this planet with us, all that we do as people is meaningless. I met people and professors who inspired me, challenged me, and got me to think beyond the human realm.

The model of the faculty was excellent in that students were required to develop their own plan of study. To identify their area of study, and the courses, projects or fieldwork that accomplished it. Our final exam was an oral examination with faculty who tested us on whether or not we had accomplished what we had set out to learn. Often as part of the plan people did a major papers, thesis, or major project. Only in retrospect do I have a sense of the freedom that the programme allowed. Courses were also pass or fail which created an atmosphere of mutual assistance.

The only solution to
fear
is
direct
action

During one of the smaller group discussions Julie, a friend of mine turned to John Livingston and said, "Well then what should I do?"

She was, I imagine at the moment, overwhelmed by the enormity of the environmental crisis and John, in his usual gruff tone replied, "I can't tell you what to do, you have to figure it our for yourself."

To which Julie responded, "But, what am I supposed to do?"

John reemphasized, "You have to figure it our for yourself."

Over the course of my studies I ran into people who would ask the same question, 'What should I do?' When they pressed me for an answer, I would respond with something equivalent to, 'Don't drive your car.'

Inevitably the response would come back, 'I can't do that,' to which I would respond, 'I told you I can't tell you what to do.'

How then, do we as educators, allow the student to find the most critical part of the subject: their desire, their inspiration, their place to make a contribution to the well being of others, their way to make a living that will nourish their soul? How do we help them connect to the part of themselves, which gathers the information, and knowledge, we are teaching them, to make it useful?

Teaching to the Student's Potential

For me, the transition to adulthood that followed high school was a challenging time. And in many ways I feel that I am just now completing that cycle.

I came again to understand those years by teaching first and second year students at York University. One of the courses I taught was called 'Environmental Thought and Literature'; it linked environmental thought and literary criticism. In it we explored different ways to see nature. The most important piece of this being the individual's perceptions—as in Quantum Physics where you cannot ignore the experimenter, in Environmental Thought you cannot ignore the perceiver. So the course was both an exploration of how different cultures perceive nature, while at the same time understanding each individual's perceptions of nature. The five years of teaching that course taught me a great deal about what students are really looking for, and what they want from the professor and the institution.

I taught the course using the model of the native medicine wheel as a thinking tool to examine the books that we read. I had discovered it during my studies, and wanted a system for thinking that I could share with the students. It was also, appropriately, 'from the land.' In the first few years I didn't make good use of this tool. Just introducing it at the beginning and then coming back to it much later in the year. Over the years, however, I got much better at weaving its lessons into the class. By the third year it struck me that it was a revelation for many students that emotion, not just thoughts, are a part of writing a good essay. That it is actually their own individual feelings which determine which thoughts they put in the essay, their order, and the style of presentation.

Each year I included some experiential components in the course. It ranged from meditation, a hike, a camping trip and one year, six of the students and I built and shared the experience of a sweat lodge. And over the years it became obvious that the students wanted to learn about the information in relationship to who they were.

Reflection and Knowledge Acquisition

The university, I perceived, was for many of them a place to cross the imaginary line between childhood and adulthood. A pause in their life, a stepping out of the stream to reflect on where they wanted to go. A time to explore in ways not thought of before—and yet, contradictorily, at the same time a place to get the skills and credentials to 'be something.' Because school helps to do both these things, acting as a source of information for future work, and a place for time-out and reflection, students often don't do either successfully.

The first component, 'time out and reflection' must be accomplished first. And once they have taken their 'time out' and emerged from it with a sense of self, students are ready to embrace the acquisition of information and to choose a direction. But to do both of these at the same time is confusing and counter-productive.

Furthermore, the university and the educational system itself are not designed for these dual purposes. The system asks the simple question: What do you want to study? And students are supposed to answer something intelligent—something that will help get them a career, or at least a job.

Redesigning the System

One year I was hired to take over a course on Critical Television half way through the class. I spent my Christmas vacation reading the articles outlined by the professor. They were articles on high-definition television, technical journals, license agreements, etc. and all I remember now from most of those readings was being bored and uninterested by them.

In the end, I decided to be honest and ask the class what interested them from the first term. They replied that they were not all that taken with the readings or the direction of the past term. Knowing that it was best to enter with my own plan, I had already created a schedule for them based on the readings I found interesting. When I outlined this plan they were relieved and excited. We went on to have a memorable half-year together. It is crucial, I learned, to ask rather than assume, and to follow my own intuition—no matter what.

In Mind Not in Body

Schools, curriculum, courses are usually designed with the student in 'mind' not in 'body'. Once the structure has been set up, and the student and teacher arrive in body, it is necessary to recognize who is there and why. It is time for the teacher to get out of his, or her plan, and into the class with the students who have arrived.

When the teacher steps out from behind the mask of information for the sake of information, the student will show himself or herself. And learning can begin. Living education seeks to bring what we are learning to the here and now, honouring the reality of what is. To honour who we are, where we are, what desires each one of us has at this time.

Making Education Live

By the time I arrived at university, I was interested in learning, which was a great gift. But along the path I had forgotten the simple question of, 'What do I want to do?' It seemed more a question of 'What am I supposed to take to get me where I am going'. And I naively thought that I was supposed to know the answer. How could I have known that the best advice would be if you don't know - don't pretend that you do.

The real question, 'What do I want?' is not accessible by my thoughts; the answers lie in my heart, feelings, and desire. It comes back to the simple questions of "Who am I?" and "What am I giving back to society?" The challenge is trusting the journey from my head which asks the question, to my heart which answers it.

Learning comes to life when the teachers, the professors, the instructors recognize where the students are and begin teaching to their potential rather than to their stated needs, or the course requirements. When the student's possibilities are not given a place to be expressed, they become erased.

My friend Julie, a yoga teacher, for a long time believed that it was hard to teach people to do headstands in just one class, and it always proved to be so. Only one out of a group of twenty would attempt it and succeed. Then one day, she decided that it was easy to teach headstands in just one class and that day all but a couple of people succeeded in doing headstands.

If it is not in the present moment, then where is it? If a group has assembled to 'learn' and a person has been appointed to 'teach' them, then what could be the next most obvious move? Those two parties meet in real life, they meet in a "class" and do they continue to be 'made up' and treated as if they weren't there? Or does that 'teacher' look at those 'students' as living people who have agreed to come together to learn something at this time… now?

A living institution recognizes that students may come for something more than what is in the course handbook. It allows for flexibility in the teaching of curriculum to make a space for teachers and students, or leaders and led, to meet.

Making education live means designing these elements into the presentation of information. Allowing the students to consider what they will use it for in the future, and how it is important to them. It requires faculty secure enough in themselves to offer students these possibilities.

Students mostly learn from each other; they carry the knowledge of the times, that teachers are not capable of knowing. This can only be shared in the context of what the teachers know, as long as the teacher is willing to facilitate the discussion. Hopefully the teacher has the ability to get the students to explore their own potential—and encourage them to open up and talk to each other.

If I could put one practice into any classroom it would be meditation or reflection. It is only in being open to the possibilities that the answers come. After all, we are a community of people sharing a consciousness and sharing a planet.

The people teaching must learn to take factors into account, which have nothing to do with their own discipline. Otherwise, they are not teaching the students in front of them—but teaching to a concept of 'student', a generalization which does not exist. Over time, students, teachers, society and institutions change; flexibility helps them connect.

The Key

The key to making education live lies in you, in me, and in everyone else. The students are individuals, and so are the teachers, facilitators, leaders, and coaches. The theories and methods are not. We each have our own way. That is the way it is supposed to be. And each one of us has to ask the question—how?

How do I bring life to what I do, here and now? The answers will be as varied as those asking. But there will be certain similarities, for the subject is always the same—life.

Find magic, and so will they.

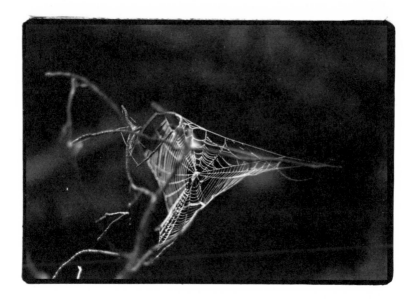

Seven Practices

The seven practices that follow are a system of engaging with yourself, your students, the material and the world. Systems, and the practices that make them real are important. They help to ensure that all the pieces of what you are doing are included in your approach.

self – world – limits – spiritual – physical – emotional – intellectual

First – breathe
Second – include your surroundings.
Third – go beyond your borders
The Fourth through Seventh are the four directions of the Teaching Wheel – East, South, West, and North – and with them, at the level of human experience, the spiritual, physical, emotional, and intellectual ways of perceiving.

That is the whole summed up. . . enjoy exploring the possibilities.

We are all in this together—you drink my water, I breathe your air. There is only one subject—life in all of its manifestations.

The Practice
of Process

Imagine that you are wandering along a path in the forest. You feel a sense of anticipation. Something lies ahead. Are you trusting, are you wary, are you filled with joy?

The way in which you approach your subject is crucial. Studies have shown that when a teacher believes that a certain student or a whole class is gifted, they excel. And when a teacher believes the reverse—that the students are not bright—they do not do well.

So, the first piece is the attitude, assumptions and manner with which you approach both the students and the subject together.

The practice section that follows suggests one approach; when you feel confident, you will be inspired to create your own.

Some languages are hard-wired to understand things, others to understand process. English is a noun-heavy, verb-poor language. We live and think in a world where

When I was guiding canoe trips I learnt that it is not what you say, but what you do that people 'see.'

No matter how many times I said, "It is important for you to wear your shoes!" If I did not wear mine, they did not wear theirs.

things matter—how they got here, where they are going. English is excellent for understanding history, but not so good for explaining the theory of relativity.

Hopi, and other aboriginal languages, are verb-rich, noun-poor. Existence is about process, relationship, action, result, energetic quality. A Hopi would be hard-pressed to see time as flowing from past to present. Explaining history would be a challenge, but a hopi child would easily grasp the four dimension of space-time as described in the theory of relativity.

Imagine that your students will not understand one word of what you say in a day. How would you set up the class to teach them something anyway? If you can do that-if you can set the process up in such a way as to convey the important elements of your class—they will 'get it,' they will remember it, and they will be able to use the information themselves. And yet I can feel as I write this that you are thinking, "but that is all that the class is about-what we are learning, the information". And I say the information is part of what they are learning. The other part is how to learn, how to think, how to write, how to present. So make sure that you are setting a good example on these issues, for as you do, you will also inspire their acquisition of information.

The only way out is through.

1. Self

"By deliberately changing the internal image of reality, people can change the world."
~: **Willis Harman**

Now. Now. Now.

There is no more powerful moment, time, inspiration, place or thought than the power of the now. Whole spiritual schools have sprung up from the simplest of practices to assist us in being present: from the Buddhists we learn to be aware of our breath; a Sioux shaman might lead us on a vision quest. At root it all comes down to being in this moment.

So, please, just be here now. Today, in the seat in which you sit, with the ways that you perceive. And encourage those whom you meet to also be present. Work in the now. For now contains all the moments of the past, future, and present, in a way that the future and the past do not.

The ego does not like the now—ego thrives on its plans for the future and its victories of the past, real or imagined—it does not differentiate.

Be present, be in the presence of others.

First Practice

Before you begin a class, sit for 5–60 minutes. Begin by following your breath. Relax. Let yourself be at one with your universe. Feel confident and comfortable with who you are and what you know. That is the foundation. Then, once you have gotten to that spot, imagine what will happen in your class. Feel the flow of the information, the ideas, the growth.

Let any creative ideas for its implementation come to you.

2. World

"To see a world in a grain of sand and a heaven in a wild flower,
Hold infinity in the palm of your hand and eternity in an hour."
~: William Blake

Show and Tell Your World

Whatever the subject you are teaching, it is your experience, your stories, your way of making the subject real that the students are interested in, because they are wondering how they can use it in their life. They may find from your stories that they are not the same as you; they may find that they are inspired to pursue other paths, but the passion woven into the learning will guide them along the way. It is really the only thing that will guide them. The information itself does not have life, it may be forgotten, they will remember the passion.

So tell stories, invite everyone to tell stories—they bring in the wisdom, they create the community. Stories can make a small space feel like it contains the whole world.

The only gift that you bring is your self. Share your gifts, your challenges, your confusion and most importantly show yourself as a person. All students want to find the person who works to engage the material.

Second Practice

As you prepare the material for a class, ask yourself how you have used the information, or how you have seen others using it. Consider the ways that your students might put it into practice. Incorporate those ideas into the presentation of the material.

If you are able, create or find an exercise, a game, a problem to solve that brings the information together with the students' own life. That is what brings the information to life.

3. Limits

"The ancients—with their gorgons, unicorns, and sphinxes—imagined more than existed, whereas moderns cannot even imagine so much as exists."
~: **Henry David Thoreau**

Into the Unknown

Beyond the world you know, there are worlds you have not imagined. We do not see beyond the boundaries of what we think is possible. When the aborigines first encountered whites, they did not see the ships out on the ocean. Their belief structure did not hold it possible that there would be something out there.

I run drum-making workshops. I tend to be a fairly laissez-faire leader. While at first I would tell students exactly how to string their drum, later I began telling them what the stringing had to accomplish. Often I was amazed and surprised by the creative approaches that students took to putting their drums together. Now I have learned that if you can address what is necessary you will find amazing results-often ones you could never have imagined yourself.

As best as you are able, set out what is required. Allow the students to create the how-to. The freedom in the how-to sections will bring the enthusiasm and energy to drive the process.

Imagine the unimaginable—if you can not imagine it—allow the space for others to imagine it.

Third Practice

Imagine the possibilities that the information you are presenting could lead to—new inventions for flight or overcoming fear, new revolutions of thought, new practices in organizations. Think up examples from the past, the internet in the past twenty years, the automobile and the airplane in the past hundred, the hybrid car in the past ten. Highlight that the new ideas of the future will be equally as unexpected.

What Russian could have imagined communism and then capitalism? The ways of the world have been myriad, magical, and unimaginable.

Allow space for your students to dream and imagine tomorrow's worlds. Get over your fear of what is not here and now. Your fear will limit your students' ability to imagine the possibilities of the world.

A circle is a universal symbol of unity.
The whole universe is made up of 'wheels'.

The Teaching Wheel

The Medicine Wheel – Heymetosts Storm
The Great Mandala (The Wheel of Life) – Buddha
The Nutrient Cycle – Albert Lineus
The Space-Time Continuum – Albert Einstein

I had been using the idea of the teaching wheel for many years. One day I decided to do a search on the internet. I found a reference to the Buddha's first teaching in Sarnath, India. His teaching was about The Dhammacakka, Dhamma is "truth" or "nature" and Cakka is translated as "wheel" or "blessing". This "Teaching Wheel", or "Truth Blessing" was represented by a wheel with 8 spokes representing the noble eightfold path for the first 400 years of Buddhism. Only in the 1st centure B.C.E. was it replaced by the Buddha figure we know today. I use the idea of the circle as a metaphor for life, for understanding the interconnectedness of life as a first principle of wholisitc thinking.

For me, the important skill is learning to adopt the metaphorical elements of the circle into your thinking process.

In order to contemplate the world in which we live a shared approach is necessary. The language we speak is only a rudimentary beginning. Using a thinking tool–an intellectual map–helps past this stage.

This map is simple, with the ability to incorporate complexity. Austere so that a child may understand, sophisticated so that one who wishes to delve into the interconnectedness of existence can explore.

Put a circle of stones on the ground.
Draw a circle on a piece of paper.
Walk in a circle.
Watch the sun rise and set and rise again.
Watch the leaves fall off a tree and return to the soil.

Simple—so that you may devote yourself to being in the world, rather than learning the system itself.

Spend your energy learning the system, rather than thinking, feeling, experiencing, and your system is too complex. A simple foundation, with the ability to explore the depths of consciousness in a universe that may contain more galaxies than grains of sand upon the earth.

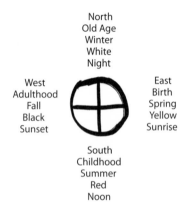

North
Old Age
Winter
White
Night

West
Adulthood
Fall
Black
Sunset

East
Birth
Spring
Yellow
Sunrise

South
Childhood
Summer
Red
Noon

A circle with 4 cardinal points-—north, south, east and west. The circle represents all of creation—things material and things immaterial; all beings sentient and non-sentient. It is also the myriad ways of perceiving. The wheel is your life: birth–child–adult–old age–death; it is a day: morning–noon–evening–night; it is the seasons spring–summer–fall–winter. It represents the stars in the sky, and the galaxies too numerous to imagine. This teaching wheel is the ultimate metaphor–inclusive, accepting, all-encompassing.

At the level of perception the wheel's magic emerges. Imagine standing with a group of people in a circle; place a stone at its center. Each one of you sees it differently. To begin you each stand in a different spot (physical level of perception, south). You have also had different individual experiences leading up to this moment, so you have different associations with stones in general (emotional understanding, west). Because of these factors you have different thoughts running through your head (the intellectual, north). Finally, from these different perceptions you have your own sense of how that stone, and stones in general, connect to life (spiritual, east) Now, consider that the 'truth' about the stone is the sum of those different perceptions within yourself and among the group.

We each have a first way of perceiving. Some will perceive an object, or event, with their heart, others with their head, or spirit, or senses. Growth comes by recognizing the different aspects of perception within yourself and among others. You grow most in understanding by perceiving from your weakest perceptual ability.

The circle rules, it turns, it reminds, it brings you back to yourself, and it gently asks what does everyone else perceive. We live on a round planet, with the elements circulating among us, we spin through the universe as universes are spun into existence. A whirling, twirling journey with change as the only constant. Use the wheel in the ways that make sense to you, be imaginative, talk to others, get your students to think in an inclusive circle.

The ideas that follow in the sections on each of the four directions are not explanations about the directions themselves. They are ways of teaching, leading, facilitating, thinking and being that have assisted me to teach, and learn, in a different manner.

May they be gifts to you.

intellect

emotion **spirit**

physical

AIR

SPIRIT

EAGLE

SUNRISE

BIRTH

YELLOW

ORANGE

SPRING

ENLIGHTENMENT

4
The Eastern Gate
The Inward Path

"I have always known that at last I would take this road,
but yesterday I did not know that it would be today."

~: Narihara :~

Walk through the Eastern Gate
with these words on your lips:

Ohm Mani Padme Hum

Which, translated from the Tibetan means,
'The world is as it should be'.

Choose the world you desire to live in.
Invite it. That is the important thing.
Then have the courage to share that world.
Watch the sunrise, watch the moonrise.
Begin each day as your first, and your last.

Black Elk Speaks 1933

"You have noticed that everything an Indian does is in a circle, and that is because the power of the world always works in circles, and everything tries to be round. . . .

Everything the power of the world does , is done in a circle. The sky is round, and I have heard that the earth is round like a ball, and so are all the stars. The sun comes forth and goes down again in a circle. The moon does the same, and both are round. Even the seasons form a great circle in their changing, and always come back again to where they were. The life of a man is a circle from childhood to childhood, and so it is in everything where power moves."

Nick Black Elk

Circle

The power of the circle
as a teaching tool is immense.
In a single gesture,
it puts existence into perspective.

Bring someone to a circle,
show them
that all of their life
is represented by that one circle.
Walk around it once, and then again.
You will have
someone who is learning
to respect the moment,
themselves and others.

Youth Talking

One day while I was working with a Cambodian youth group in Toronto, I had them pass a talking stick around a circle. The first time around, many held it and said nothing. The second time they held it for a bit longer, recognizing that they actually had the attention of the others. The third time around, those who did not speak at the beginning began to speak; aware that they were heard. And from their words, the circle became complete.

All had now committed to be present. Each person had seen some of the soul of the other. The fourth and fifth times around contained moments of magic. At the end of the talk I told them about a sweat lodge, and they were keenly interested. It felt as if some sense of spirit, hidden at the beginning, had awoken within the group.

> *"The inner world is as large as the outer world"*
> *R.D. Laing*

The Inward Path

Each person that sits before you, each
seasonal or seasoned lecturer, each
flower, each sunrise, says,

"Yes, it is possible to be renewed!"

Offer back to them what their spirit says
and what their past experiences may not
have offered, that which their friends
and family may have fled.

Invite their spirit on a journey.

Make an offering: a seed, a song, a
story—these things call to the spirit.
Honour that they are capable of
greatness and assist them to see the fire
within.

Each person I have met rises
enthusiastically to the challenge of
being potent, present, courageous and
inspired.

We may not be a spiritual society;
yet we are spirit.

Coming Together

I set out the map and pointed to a route I had been thinking of which was twice the regular length of a week-long canoe trip. I said I had heard it was a beautiful route, and it would be quite deserted, for few attempt the seven portages up Maple Creek to Maple Lake, in the north-west corner of Algonquin Park. The group agreed to try it.

For lunch on the first day we stopped on an outcropping of rock in the gentle waters of the Amable De Fond River. I pointed out the menu and told everyone where to find the ingredients, the pots etc.

"Whoever wishes to cook is welcome to," I said and added, "If you cook you don't have to wash the dishes."

We ate peanut butter, jam, cheese, cucumber, tomato and pita, then lay back for a short rest on the warm rocks before continuing to North T Lake. By the next evening we had reached the bottom of Maple Creek, where we camped and swam in the warm water. After dinner, some of us went for a paddle, and for the first time I noticed the reflection of stars on the calm, black lake.

We started out early the next morning, and struggled up those portages.

I remember Ken, my fourteen-year-old assistant, carrying a canoe up a steep hill saying, "Energy creates energy," as he passed me by.

Inspiration makes what is difficult, into an adventure. Adventure brings people together.

I can picture a swampy place where we debated whether or not to drink the water. We worked well together and arrived early in the evening at the lake spread out before us, water high up on the Algonquin dome of the Canadian Shield.

We arrived at our campsite near dark. Content, tired, somehow we made dinner, and sat around reveling in our accomplishment.

We made mint tea with mint we had gathered on the river. And we added hot chocolate to it—discovering mint hot chocolate.

I felt the coming together of the group at the beginning when we all looked at the map as 'individuals' considering the route plan. This opened the possibility for us to work together. We each consented to a mutual purpose, with inspiration and a sense of adventure, creating a group where before had been individuals. We could be ourselves, and we could be one. I enjoyed the working together of the group—so did they.

Inspiration

There is only one thing you can hope
to kindle in the life of another:
the spark that they carry.

Give it light and air to grow with,
and you will have a student ready for adventure.
That student will know the challenge
is their own, as are the rewards.

"Inspiration makes what
is difficult into an adventure.
Adventure brings people together."

Vision Quest

Upon finishing my Master's degree, I felt that it was time to move into the next stage of me, hence the idea to do a vision quest.

'O, Great Spirit, have mercy on me that my people may live.' I repeated those words from The Book of the Vision Quest through much of my four days with no food and little water. I sat on a rock, surrounded by forest, above the Magnetawan River, which flows off the Algonquin dome—the Canadian Shield, some of the oldest rock in the world—down to Georgian Bay and then out to the ocean.

I slept in a hammock under a buffalo coat. I lay around, I napped, I sat. I played my drum and my recorder. Once a day I walked and canoed to a rock where I left a note for my partner. For me, the time spent being with myself in the wild was both powerful and humbling. I got back to the basics, back to me, back to my body.

A day, or a moment of reflection, can bring clarity to years of work. I did not see any spirits come to tell me what to do—I saw myself, and my potential.

There's a native saying, "If the men in a society are not initiated into it, they will destroy it."

Walking back on that fourth day, empty, light-headed, grateful for friends and food, I felt a deep love for all things. I felt that nature had washed over and through me and now I was clear.

The words, 'O, Great Spirit, have mercy on me that my people may live,' subtly changed their meaning over those days. I went from the feeling that I was somehow supposed to change and help my society to the sense that I am a part of something larger, and that the something larger is important to me. I came back feeling that the day-to-day world and the spiritual are the same. I could feel spirit in everywhere. Somehow the details of living daily life had led me to believe that I had to search out spirit, when really spirit is everywhere, in everything, always. All I have to do is open up and perceive, be aware, feel, see, hear, be in the wild and know that it is all a part of spirit.

Since then, I have done other vision quests and mostly, I have learned to appreciate spirit and possibility in every moment. A day, or a moment, of reflection can bring clarity to years of work. Nature is always here. I am always here, possibility and potential are always here.

More clarity, faith, determination, hope, love, patience, simplicity is always welcome.

Initiation

Learning is about moving
from one place in your life to the next.
You meet with a group of people,
learn information, and explore it
in relationship to yourself
to get to your next level.

All too often dimensions of who you are,
who you could be, and what is possible for you
are left out of the picture.

Education is about becoming a part of society.
It is about taking responsibility for the whole,
as best as you are able. It requires you to shine
your light, joy and love where you are able.

Living Is Creating
"The material made sense to us because we lived in it."

At York University I taught a course called 'Technology, Magic & Ritual'. The course was an exploration of the rituals in our lives, looking at rituals and habits to discover our beliefs about the world. We considered two basic ways of understanding: technology and magic.

Someone with a technological view of the world may have a cup of coffee to begin the day because it starts up the body, whereas someone with a sacred, or magical, world view—where everything is connected to everything else—may say a prayer.

I structured the class to mimic the topic, and began the year with my djembe drum, playing to begin and end the first class. To "open" and "close" the second class, we smudged with sweet-grass. For the rest of the year, individual students took turns opening and closing the class. This was a great part of the anticipation, as something new was presented each week.

Three years after the course took place, I got a letter from one of the students, who wrote, "…even now I consider myself blessed for having been part of that year. For I imagine what I would be like today without having taken your class—and I do not like what I see."

I have often reflected on what he meant and what we learned in that class: to be present. To see each other, ourselves, and to see how things are interconnected. That was our magic.

In the process, I experienced that to really learn material, it is best to mimic the way in which it is learnt with the process itself. 'Ceremony', as I call it, or 'structure', is the way in which you create the learning environment. The material made sense to us because we lived in it.

Ceremony

I consider every class to be a ceremony.

The basic elements of a ceremony are the beginning, the middle and the end. It is that simple. Like walking into a temple, being in it, and then leaving. At the beginning, call in the energy, feeling, sense, that you wish to be present. Then have fun with it and at the end, thank what you called in, and let it return to where it came from.

You call energy in whatever form makes sense to you. It could be your grandmother; it could be your ability to run well, whatever is strength for you. It is the way you connect to your centre. That is where you are strong, that is where you are whole and effective. Allow yourself to be in that place, to remember in your body what it is like to be there.

Ceremonies, like advertising,
develop power by repetition.
By repeating a ceremony,
a group of people come to
their own sacred space and time.
With repetition they learn
better and better
how to get there quicker.

Awareness

The greatest way to change
the way someone is, acts, feels,
is to shine the light of you
out into the world,
doing, being what you are.

Let people change for themselves.
Your true self is the inspiration that lights
the way for others.

We are all intelligent, and capable of being ourselves,
and that is something to remember.

If you want to be patient, feel your impatience.
If you want peace, feel your strength.

Five Minutes
People want to experience themselves

At York University, one of my classes had a component on Eastern philosophy. I told the students that meditation is an important component of how the world is perceived in the East—and I suggested that, as well as talking about Eastern philosophy, we try meditation.

The students agreed, so we reserved a room with a carpeted floor, and for five minutes we focused on our breath. Some sat on the floor, others on chairs.

"Keep your back straight," I said. "Focus on your breath, notice any thoughts and let them go, just sit and pay attention to your breath."

Before we started, I told them that if someone felt uncomfortable trying this they were welcome to not participate. In five years, not one student chose to sit out.

At the end of each year, I asked students on the evaluation form which class stood out. At times almost half of them would recount the class where we meditated. The five minutes of not thinking, of not talking, held more weight than any idea, concept or thought in twenty-six weeks of ideas, concepts and information. Many of them also mentioned the day we sat outside on the grass, or the hike we took.

I experienced the same thing recently when I led a five-day drum-making class at the Haliburton School of the Arts. On the first day we did a twenty minute drum journey. At the end of the week, many of the people recalled those twenty minutes as memorable among the five days of talking, playing and making drums. It seems that I can not learn this lesson too many times: people want new and unique experiences.

When you are estranged from yourself, you are the most interesting of subjects. Experience of yourself is the most memorable of lessons.

Enlightenment

Often there is an energetic jump
from one moment to the next.
It is as if new information just entered
and made greater awareness possible.

Notice it.

That is enlightenment.

Letting Go

A vision quest is a death—you have to let go of the old self in order to welcome the new. Every new day is a birth, a renewal; each moment releases all the moments that have gone before. I often send a group of students back into the hall, and ask them to make a conscious choice to be in the class, allowing them to decide what they want from it, from themselves, and from me.

They return renewed with a better understanding about what they are doing than they may have had when they signed up for the class.

Endings are Beginnings

To perceive differently,
get out of the world that is familiar.
Leave what you know,
allow possibility, make space,
get a view of the larger landscape.

Entering the world as a baby
is one of our greatest challenges,
scary, cold, different,
yet we must leave the protected world
in order to grow.

You never do know exactly
where you will end up.

We have all been encouraged
to keep ourselves a secret,
even from ourselves!

EARTH

BODY

MOUSE

NOON

CHILDHOOD

RED

GREEN

SUMMER

INNOCENCE

5
The Southern Gate

Be a gift to yourself.
Learn with your body.
From all of your experiences,
with all of your senses, you grow.
Experience this present piece of your journey.
You are your gift to the world.

Be a gift to yourself.
Calm the critic. Love your journey.
Any judgment of its goodness or not-so-goodness
just gets in the way of you
being you.
Have the courage, patience, and wisdom
to say nothing more often.

Listen

There once was a Chinese man who had a horse.
One day the horse ran away.
His neighbour said, "Oh, that is terrible!"
The man responded, "Maybe, maybe not."
The next day the horse came back with another horse.
The neighbour commented, "How lucky you are!"
The man responded, "Maybe, maybe not."

The man's son went to ride the newly-acquired horse.
He was thrown and broke his leg.
The opinionated neighbour commented, "What a tragedy!"
Again the man responded, "Maybe, maybe not."

A few weeks later, the army came to conscript
all the young men of the village;
the man's son was left behind
because of his broken leg.

The neighbour said nothing.

Start at the Beginning

Invite introductions.
Recognize the people present.

Who are you?
What are you doing here, and why?
Who are the students?
What are they doing here and why?

How?
Be as honest as possible.
Only by beginning where we are
will we get anywhere that matters.
Pretend you are interested
in teaching when you are not,
and the students will pretend
that they are interested in learning.
It is that simple.

And, of course, the beginning
contains the ending.
Where are we going, and why?
Decide on that, and agree on it,
then you have power, possibility,
shared inspiration, direction
and commitment.
And all are included.

Merging Worlds

Try this:

Hold out your two hands,
palms facing up.

In one, put all that talks about life;
in the other, put all that talks about education.

Now clap them together!

You have just joined these two worlds.

Techniques

The underlying dimension of technique is to allow the group energy to flow in a circle. If it is not flowing, your job is to ask why and to get it flowing again. The following are some of the ways to help it along.

Opening & Closing

I often think of openings and closings as the bookends that hold a class together. Something fun at the beginning, like a story or a song, encourages people to get there on time. And ending on a high note leaves people looking forward to the next class.

Breathing

The foundation for meditation (as well as living) is breath. In the awareness of breath going in and out lies a lifetime of understanding, and awareness of breath brings people into the present.

Discussion

Encourage people to talk. One method I often use is: think, write, pair, discuss. 'Pair' means to talk to the person next to you before opening up the discussion for the whole group. Discussion should be used with other techniques to complete the circle, to bring what we know on the inside to the outside.

Storytelling

You carry stories of your life. In them lies your power and your lessons. Tell them, and encourage others to tell theirs. A great deal of power comes from retelling them. Stories also help bring facts and information together, and give them meaning. Use a story at the beginning of a class to sum up what people will do with the information that they receive

Talking Stick

An object that, when held, gives the speaker the group's complete attention without interruption until the speaker is finished, at which point the speaker passes the 'stick' to the next person. The speaker can choose to sit and think as part of their talking, or silently pass the stick on. It was used by many of the native north american tribes and many other cultures across the globe.

Movement

Means 'moving around.' Body positions greatly affect our learning: 'our brains can only absorb what our bottoms will endure.' It can be as easy as stretching or extend to playing games. In an outdoor experiential setting, it may be trust falls; in a classroom, it could be getting up for a stretch and coffee break. No matter what age, level or subject, movement is crucial.

Silence, Dreaming & Reflection

This is the real source of education. Creating opportunities for people to connect to their underlying reasons for living gives information meaning. Even in an economics class each person has a different reason for being there—help them know why they are there and they will be interested and present.

I use guided meditations, guided drum journeys, meditation, writing exercises, and anything else I can dream up to get people to dream and reflect.

Role Playing

Try out what you are talking about, play with it. Be the characters, stand in their shoes, recall their ideas. Play out the scene from history, rediscover the North Pole. Have fun with it.

Drumming

I first used drums in a class to offer students the experience of a drum-journey. Drums are excellent for giving people a non-linguistic way to communicate.

Drawing

Using pen, ink, colour, paint, paper, allows you to see parts of yourself that are hard to see without putting them on paper. Drawing is an excellent technique used in conjunction with dreaming and reflection. It allows people to express ideas in a non-linear way.

Ceremony

A created ritual with an intent and a purpose. It can also be considered as the structure within which the group meets. A way of beginning and ending, a way of conducting the process. It is the emotional/intellectual/spirit space in which people meet.

WATCH THE CENTRE

Those that occupy centre stage
hold the group energy.
Put mechanisms in place so that it
is held in a balanced fashion.

Working with a Group

Show them where attention is required.

A group of people who come together to learn want to do what is required in order to learn. Show them where attention is required. Show them what you know: how to light a fire or cook on it, how to carry a canoe, how to stay warm at night. Show them how you have learned to appreciate the trees, and rivers and sunsets.

As they recognize what needs doing, they will do it. As they collect meaning from the day, watch them, smile. As they stop asking you questions, feel your freedom, your lack of need for control, and your respect for their ability.

At first, more effort is required to organize, and later, more effort is required to let go and do what you love.

Teaching and leading
are not life
they are nurturing life,
at times, it is necessary.

Follow the Stars, Walk on the Ground

If you can point out the stars, and the sky, and the mountains in the distance, and point out that there is much more out there than we can see from our present location, then people will be inspired, and they will be present.

If the field is small and made up of information, then the students will be full of information, and not be themselves.

Real leading is always and only about each one of us finding ourselves. There is only one subject—your own life. Our entire universe is contained in the seed that is you.

How?

Sing
Drum
Dance
Pray
Play
Laugh
Read
Talk
Walk
Argue
Get Dirty
Get Wet
Think
Do Nothing
Do Anything
Draw
Act
Sweat
Get Bored
Get Inspired
Sit
Run
Dream
Be Honest
Smile

Now!

Power

Live in your centre.

There is only one place to be—here and now.
If you are here, then you are in your power.
If you are not here—you are nowhere.
Your power comes from who you are.

And who you are comes
from what you feel, and think, and perceive.
And what you feel comes from what you do.

And what you do
creates inspiration and perspiration,
which creates who you are.

Be able to do nothing with grace and love.

You Just Have to Experience It

I began to meditate when I was five or six. I would lie in bed with a paradoxical sensation—something large, and something small, each somehow separate, and also part of the same thing. It felt like an endless circle beyond words. I remember a similar sensation sitting in the Sinai Desert on the shores of the Red Sea; as I looked up at the stars, the boundary between the stars and me, vanished. I sat on the sand, on the surface of earth—a large rock floating in space, me, stars, earth, sand, all a part of the same interconnected ocean.

As a child, I also remember wondering about my mother's death, which happened when I was four. I remember the thoughts clearly: 'I like who I am… I'd be different if she were alive… I guess that her death is a part of the way things are supposed to be.' There you have it, my foundation for meditation: a deep acceptance of what is.

When I lived in Jerusalem I found the book that taught me meditation in the classical sense: *Zen Mind, Beginners Mind* by Shunryu Suzuki. Simple, wise. Zen-style meditation: pay attention to your breath, sit with your back straight, watch thoughts pass, let them go.

It seemed already a part of me. I'd meditate before going to sleep and when I awoke. Often during meditation a sensation of being part of everything settled in.

I gave *Zen Mind* to my ninety-five year-old grandmother—who has a Ph.D. and read five books a week. She read it, and summed it up with a classic western-dualism-meets-eastern-mysticism comment: "Is he crazy? What does he mean by: 'You die, and you don't die'?"

Meditation was never meant to be understood by rational thought. You just have to experience it.

Meditation

Follow your breath.

Work towards meditating
for twenty minutes at a time.
Start with what is comfortable.

Meditation is like entering a new reality.
At first it seems there is nothing there.
After looking in the door long enough, it is
obvious that there is something.

Still, it takes time to adjust
one's senses to perceive it.
So, be patient, persistent
and understanding with yourself.

Sitting, Moving

In my class at York University, after a few months of habit had worked its way into our class and seating position was assumed, I got students to change where they were sitting.

When explaining Taoism, I got them to try out a tai chi exercise: you hold yourself rigid and someone tries to push you over. Then you let yourself be relaxed and repeat the same exercise, and you find that the energy goes by you. In this way, one experiences that strength comes from flexibility and that being rigid is not as strong.

In another class, we created our own medicine wheels on the floor with stones, and then sat in the centre of them. Inside the wheels we got a sense of who we are. We jumped out of the circles recognizing our ability to change. We gathered the stones together with the knowledge that at every moment we recreate ourselves.

Often I bring people outside, sometimes to sit on the grass and talk, at other times to walk and look around. We have much more to talk about when we get back from one of those journeys.

Movement & Body

Get up, walk around.
Look at each other.
This makes all the difference.

Find a way to walk around the subject...
to play with it...

with your:
fingers,
legs,
stomach,
neck,
back,
knees,
feet.

Dance is movement,
any kind.

The more your body is involved,
the more present you are with whatever you are:
doing, learning, feeling, digesting.

Get outside, change rooms, clear the static,
brush it off you and your students.
Bend, stretch, laugh.
Breathe.

WATER

EMOTION

BEAR

EVENING

ADULTHOOD

BLACK

BLUE

FALL

INTUITION

6

The Western Gate
Holding Heart Space

Your heart—Follow it.
It is in your body; connect to it
and you will lead a life of beauty.
Ask, and when the answer is clouded,
be patient.
When tears come, thank them.
Let them flow. When ego interferes,
let it speak its piece, thank it, let it go.

Above the door of the temple at
Delphi is written:
'Know thyself.'

Opening Yourself, Just by Doing It

When I was four years old, my mother died unexpectedly. My parents were visiting her brother on his coconut plantation on the Pacific coast of Mexico. My brother and I were left at home, in the care of an old woman we did not know. I remember helping her to find her glasses one morning—she couldn't see without them.

The night my father came back I went to the top of the stairs. I remember seeing my uncle and aunt, the suitcases, my father. I sat on the wood at the top of the stairs. I remember being small. The large wooden banister beside me...the stairs a long way down...

I called down, "Where's mommy?"

My dad responded, "I'll be up in a minute."

I went back to my bed. He came up and sat beside me on the bed. "Mommy died, she's not coming back," he said. And he gave me a shell—small, conical and pointy. I

The heart has its reasons that reason does not know.
Blaise Pascal

felt a tear coming. I felt something large and sad. The words didn't have much meaning for me. I cried a bit.

What is death? I wondered. Perhaps it's like sleep, I thought. Then the thought entered my mind: in sleep you dream. I knew this was different—she was not asleep. She felt further away than that. Life went on. I don't know what else I thought; it was the way it was.

From then on, my Bubbie (Yiddish for grandmother), her mother, considered my brother and me her children. We spent winter holidays and summers with her. She would often confuse our names with her sons'. She taught me how to hug, how to be silent and how to tell stories just by doing it. Only recently has it dawned on me that some part of me knows that my mother still exists. Even if I didn't know how or where.

I had to open up to find her. Just like I have to open up to find you, or you to find me. To find each other, or the answer to a question, requires opening yourself to accept the world as it is.

Canoeing in Killarney

Once, as a canoe guide, I led a group to Killarney Provincial Park. It was August when the days are shorter, cooler, and the nights longer. There were two trips to Killarney that week, mine and one led by a guide named Michael. To me, Michael was the ideal canoe guide—a great storyteller who would double back to carry another canoe across a portage and who cooked amazing meals.

My group worked well together. We carried canoes together. We cooked together, we sang songs, and we hiked up to Silverpeak. There were three women who sang beautifully. I can still picture them paddling down the lake in unison, singing "Edelweiss" in three-part harmony. One night a small group of us stayed up 'til dawn watching the moon set in the west, and watching Mars, Jupiter and Saturn rise majestically from the lake before us. We were not well rested for the following day—but we were happy.

On the last night of the trip, as a cool August rain fell, we ended up on a little island together with Michael's group. They were complaining about the weather and the portages, and generally seemed to not be having a great trip. It was clear to me that the group had not come together. They were still individuals. Our group was content; people had carried and cooked and talked together. I lay in my hammock as supper was being prepared,

A long habit of not thinking a thing wrong, gives it a superficial appearance of being right.
Thomas Paine

resting and listening to conversations around the fire. In that half dreamy state I understood that being the star does not allow others to shine.

Doing things for people can encourage them to expect, rather than to act.

Sometimes the greatest gift is to create a space for others to step in and discover what they can contribute.

Hold The Joy

There is only one person
you can make sure has a good time.
And that is you.

You are the microcosm of the group.
Learn from your own experience
that it reflects the group experience.

If you are hungry or thirsty or tired,
there is a good chance someone else in the
group is hungry or thirsty or tired.

If you are having fun,
there is a good chance that
someone else is having fun.

Go inward to find your inspiration.
That is the gift that you offer.

Hold the space.

Let things be.

The Learning Process

I have brought university students to the woods, dragged a group of German boyscouts on the longest, hardest canoe trip of my life, and brought a group of drum-making students to play before four-hundred and fifty kids at a summer camp. I have walked four kilometers with canoes to see what was down a river for the day. I have told canoe trippers to gather seven white and seven black stones in order to hear the end of a story. I have sounded incoherent for the first part of a talk so that only the students truly interested would stay for the second half. I have burned sweetgrass and sage in community centres. I have told students in a university course called Critical Television to pay attention to how they watch television for three days, and then to not watch it for a day and compare. I have got other students to write and perform a play. In another class we wrote a book. All of this was inspired by them, or suggested by me.

And with a link to the subject we were studying they eagerly let it be a part of the learning process.

Inspiration Information

Information without inspiration is the end of learning. For information to be alive, it must be whole, and it must be connected by some story to the individual learning it.

It is the role of the teacher, the facilitator and the leader to make possible and desirable the questions, "What does this mean to me?" and "How is it part of my life?" And to leave open the door of the possibility that it may not be important for a student and that the student might walk out the door.

For that student, leaving might be a powerful reaction. Perhaps others will walk in...

Without inspiration, information is dead rather than alive. And if the information has no context for the student, it's irrelevant.

I feel that my mission is wherever I am,
to express my feeling about the importance of kindness,
compassion and the true sense of brotherhood.
I practice these things.
It gives me more happiness, more success.
If I practiced anger or jealousy or bitterness,
no doubt my smile would disappear.

~: The Dalai Lama :~

Ego

One year, I was contracted to guide a bunch of the brothers and kids of the Eaton Family (rich folk) on a three day canoe trip to Temagami.

We packed up the gear, food, and canoes, and met the family at a float-plane landing on Lake Tamagami. We flew into the top of the "Golden Staircase" and started our trip.

They expected the guides to do the cooking, to set up the tents, and to cater to their desires, something I was uninterested in. The trip was good, save the quiet tension between what they wanted and what we did and did not do for them.

The next year Michael took them out. He cooked, and carried canoes, he set up tents: he did it all. At the end of the trip they gave him a thousand dollar canoe as a tip.

Sometimes it is important to recognize that cooperation or learning is not what is desired.

Cooperation

Darwin was right, but the subsequent
misinterpretation of him was devastating.
Nature, life, business, do not work by competition.
They work by cooperation

When the people in the companies figure that out,
and Coke and Pepsi stop fighting for market share
the world will turn on its head.

Try out cooperation for a year
rather than competition,
you will sleep better, have more friends,
and people will call with thanks and appreciation
for you and your work.

Expectations

When I was taking my level two canoe tripping course one of the leaders, a man named Les, decided to teach us (a fairly seasoned bunch of canoeists) how to paddle. He figured he would treat us as if we had never done it before. He talked to us as if we were unintelligent (I think that is often how we talk to children), he told us to stay together, and be careful, not to splash each other, as he modeled a front stroke. Expecting us to watch, and learn something.

Within about fifteen minutes of him treating us this way, our group of twenty-year-olds were doing what we should not have been doing: splashing, not listening, pushing and pulling the other canoes. We must have looked like rowdy four-year-olds! And then I suddenly realized we were acting out exactly what he did not want.

We had nothing intelligent to hear-so we stopped listening. I pointed this out to the group-that we were acting just like the kids he was treating us like. We continued to do it for a bit, and then calmed down.

I learned to play in my twenties, and I'm still learning.

We do what is expected, we act the part.

So expect the best.

Trust in what you expect and ask, do it knowing that it is best for those you guide.

Be Child-Like

Do what feels right.

Children's books tell us all we need to know about the world.
Life is simple: be good, be kind, play fair,
love your neighbours, and let the younger kids play.
Later in life people get too clever to stay simple.
Life is simple. Stay with the basics.
Follow the advice offered to children.
Do what feels right.
If someone asks for something in an unkind way,
get them to say please, or ignore them,
or go play in another sandbox.
Pay attention to the small things
and the large ones will work out.

Indra and the Parade of Ants

"Indra, the king of the gods, greatly exalted after he slew the great dragon, summoned Vishvakarman, the god of arts and crafts, and commanded him to erect such a palace as would be worthy of Indra's own unequaled splendor. Vishvakarman worked very hard and in a year had succeeded in constructing a shining residence that would surely satisfy Indra. But this was not the case, for every time Indra visited this new creation, he developed visions beyond visions of new and more complicated marvels that he ordered to be added to his beautiful palace. This was understandably frustrating to our craftsman, Vishvakarman, and he decided to seek help from the creator god, Brahma. Brahma assured Vishvakarman that he would soon be relieved of his burden.

The next morning, a Brahmin boy (or holy child) appeared at the gate of Indra. The king instantly recognized the holy nature of the child and ushered him in and asked the purpose of his coming. The Brahmin boy tells Indra that he has heard of the mighty palace he is building and then comments that "no Indra before you has ever succeeded in completing such a palace as yours is to be."

Indra, full of the wine of triumph (or pride), is amused at the boy's pretense at knowledge and asks if he has seen very many Indra's come and go. The boy calmly addresses Indra, saying "Oh King of Gods, I have known the dreadful dissolution of the universe. I have seen all perish, again and again, at the end of every cycle. at that terrible time, every single atom dissolves into the primal, pure waters of eternity, whence originally all arose. Everything then goes back into the fathomless, wild infinity of the ocean, which is covered with utter darkness and is empty of every sign of animate being. Ah, who will count the universes that have passed away, or the creations that have risen afresh, again and again, from the formless abyss of the vast waters? Who will number the passing ages of the world, as they follow each other endlessly? And who will search through the wide infinities of space to count the universes side by side, each containing its Brahma, its Vishnu, its Shiva. who will count the Indras in them all--those Indras side by side, who reign at once in all the innumerable worlds; those others who passed away before them; or even the Indra's who succeed each other in any given line, ascending to godly kingship, one by one, and, one by one, passing away? King of Gods, there are among your servants certain who maintain that it may be possible to number the grains of sand on earth and the drops of rain that fall from the sky, but no one will ever number all those Indra's. This is what the Knowers know."

The boy continues to speak in this manner while, meanwhile, a parade of ants had made its appearance in the hall. This sight sets the holy child to laughing. At Indra's stammering request, he explains his action. "I laughed because of the ants. The reason is not to be told… it is the secret that smites with an ax the tree of worldly vanity, hews away at its roots, and scatters its crown." But with a great amount of humility, Indra begs the holy child to share his secret. The boy concedes and says "I saw the ants, O Indra, filing in long parade. Each was once an Indra. Like you, each by virtue of pious deeds once ascended to the rank of a king of gods. But now, through many rebirths, each has become again an ant. This army is an army of former Indras."

Brahmavaivarta Purana

When the Unexpected Happens

Ask yourself whether what is happening is o.k. or not. If it is then let it happen, and when you feel it is not so good, that is the time to step into the middle and make a shift in the direction.

True leadership is knowing when to act and when not to act.

Greek Philosophy

The use of reason to understand the world was a huge leap of Greek philosophy. The great assertion of Greek thought, made by Thales of Miletus, was that the world is made of one substance. He said that the world is made up entirely of water; that this assumption is not true is irrelevant. What this meant is that the world could be explored systematically in regards to this one substance. Before this belief, Greek thought, like all other thought, had an unknown quantity—the Gods. In the Iliad, written in the eighth or ninth century B.C.E., the Gods had a great influence upon what happened on the material plane. Arrows are turned at the last moment by a whim of the Gods; men live or die in battle depending on the wishes of the Gods.

In this God's world it should be obvious that any type of rational, logical, scientific approach is futile, for magic and knowledge 'beyond reason' reigns. Western thought is one of the few instances where humans came to believe that we are capable of knowing nature: that it is within our ability to understand it, and manipulate it to our benefit, and not suffer any unforeseen consequences. In almost any other culture the gods would first be consulted.

> *"The trick is not to rid your*
> *stomach of butterflies,*
> *but to make them fly in formation."*
> *~: Unknown*

If You Meet
the Buddha on the Road
Kill Him!

You must find your own way.
There is only one boat in which
to cross the river—your own.

Venture in another's,
and one day you will still have to get into your
own.

Only it can carry all the
dimensions of who you are.

And if you have lost it,
you will have to swim back across the sea.
And if you have never known it
you will search for the tree
from which to carve it.

FIRE

INTELLECTUAL THOUGHT

BUFFALO

NIGHT

OLD AGE

WHITE

WINTER

WISDOM

7
The Northern Gate
Thoughts are Things

Thoughts are fire
Thoughts are things.

Life is about transformation.
Everything changes, everything moves,
be aware when you get caught up believing
otherwise. Follow around the circle,
and you will know your path.

The Wood Cutter

Once upon a time there was a wood cutter. He was getting old, and it was getting hard to cut down trees, to chop them up, and to carry the wood to market. One morning he went out to pray-telling god that he needed help. Well, right before him God appeared and said He had a genie that could do all of his work for him—and lo and behold a genie appeared.

"There is one catch," said God, "If the genie has nothing to do, he'll eat you."

"Great, and thanks" said the woodcutter.

'No problem', thought the woodcutter, 'There's plenty to do!'

"How can I be of assistance?" asked the genie.

The wood cutter asked the genie to cut down a few trees, and cut them up. He went back to his little cabin, and sat on the porch to relax, gazing out at the morning. Not long after he had settled down, the genie returned, having completed his task.

"How can I be of assistance?" chirped the genie.

The wood cutter was surprised, and asked him to carry the wood to market, to sell it, and to buy some groceries.

The wood cutter sat on his porch, God's last comment that the genie would eat him if he had nothing to do now weighed heavily on his rest. He made a leisurely lunch, and just as he went out to relax there was the genie.

"How can I be of assistance?" he said.

Well, all through the afternoon and evening the woodcutter and the genie stayed awake, the wood cutter thinking up tasks, the genie asking, 'How can I be of assistance?' The wood cutter was scared and tired.

First thing in the morning, as the genie was busy cleaning the windows of the wood cutter's house, the wood cutter was out praying for God again. God appeared in front of the disheveled, exhausted wood cutter.

"Yes," said God, and the wood cutter explained his predicament. He was about to be eaten. God simply said, "When you do not have something for the genie to do, ask him to climb up and down a tree. When you need him, call him away from this, and tell him what to do."

"Thank you," said the wood cutter, who enjoyed the rest of his days.

The moral of the story is that the genie is like your mind—if it does not have something to do, it will eat you.

The Master's Master

A native friend of mine told me how people would come to her and tell her that they had learned something from their master.

She would ask them, "And with whom did your master study?"

To which they would respond reverently naming the masters master.

"And who was his master?" she would ask, until they got to the end of their ability to recite masters.

"And where do you think the first one got their knowledge?" she would ask.

"From nature." she would respond.

Each one of us has the ability to go to the real master—Nature. And to study long and hard, or slow and easy, and become masters ourselves...

My master also is nature.

Sing Yourself

Your nose is your nose, your voice is your voice. There is no point judging one or the other.

Songs, like rhythm, sit whole in our brain and body. They have a magical way of bringing the pieces together. Before the travelling minstrel's, people sang for the love of it by reusing tunes from songs they knew. There was no expert, there were no professionals, there was no proper way to sing a song.

There still isn't. Honouring those who move us with their voice is a pleasure, it is not meant to replace any of our individual voices or own songs.

You use what you have, and of course you do your best, and if you practice you will get better.

Start where you are, there is no other choice.

"Examine all you have
been told and dismiss
all that insults your soul."

~: *Walt Whitman* :~

Body & Soul

In the beginning the Creator made the universe, this earth, the mountains, oceans, lakes, rivers, the trees, plants and insects. Then God created the fish, the birds, the animals and all the other things in the sky and oceans of the earth.

Finally, the Creator created human bodies and human souls. The bodies were on earth, and the souls went up to the sky. The Creator intended the bodies and souls to be together, and so asked the souls to get into the bodies, they did not.

Time went by, and the Creator looking out over the beautiful world felt again that the bodies and souls should be together, and again asked the souls to get into the bodies, still they remained in the sky.

More time passed, and the Creator felt a bit uneasy with the separation of body and soul. This time, the Creator got angry at the souls saying, "Get into the bodies!" Still they refused.

The Creator sat back (metaphorically), realizing that a creative solution was required to unite the bodies and the souls.

So the Creator taught the bodies to drum, to dance, to sing, and to tell stories. So the bodies began to drum, to sing, to dance and to tell stories. The souls looked down, and thought, "Wow, that looks like fun!" and one by one, the souls entered into the bodies.

What we learn from this story is that it is important to drum, dance, sing, and tell stories in order to keep body and soul together.

Stories

We do not remember isolated details well. They take focus and dedication and work to put into our memory, and even after we have done that they easily slip away—but stories we remember. We can put a bunch of details into a story and we can remember it.

The reason for this is wholeness. The brain stores information in particular places, and rhythm it stores in the whole brain. So it is relatively easy to recall stories, to bring back, to reconnect the pieces. And sometimes when we do not have the particular piece that came from a story we will fetch another that fits the space.

"To know that you know what you know
and that you do not know what you do not know,
that is true knowledge."

~: *Confuscious* :~

The First Time

I begin classes in many ways. At York I started one class playing a djembe, another reading The Lorax, by Dr. Seuss. Another, I got all the students to tell what animal they felt closest to and why—I can still picture the woman who said she felt closest to a bat. One year I brought in silver dollars and we peeled away the shells, and students were instructed to take the seeds home and plant them. In a high school, I got students to begin and end class by spinning around three times.

I begin drum making workshops smudging with sweetgrass or sage. I love to tell stories, either about what happened on the way to the class, or stories that I know (and jokes!).

The first time I taught 'The Art & Spirit of Teaching', I told students about the course's creation. After planning it for three years it was finally accepted at a college for a week long summer course. The information that we were discussing was—a new way of thinking about education—what you hold in your hands is the foundation for that course. Two weeks before it was to begin, there were only four people in the class, and usually classes are cancelled with less than eight. Yet the administrator 'had a feeling' that it would be good, and wanted it to run. By the time the course took place, there were seven people in it. The building that we were given was a timber frame building on the outskirts of the college. Our subject, like our classroom was on the periphery of what was happening. Contextualizing the class' existence gave the students a way to gather the pieces of what the class was in a very real and practical way. It also served to give them a sense of where I had come from to get there.

One of the students in the class taught business writing, and she loved to write poetry.

"Start your class with a poem," I suggested, "and then explain to them how it fits in. They won't walk out, they'll be intrigued. Convince them how useful business writing is; a great business plan might one day allow them to start the business of their dreams—with a five million dollar loan."

For a time I got traditional, and started classes with explanations of what the class is about. Now I have gone back to experiences, a story rather than thoughts, a song, an animal. I've noticed, it is the silence that will be remembered.

Possibilities live in silence...

Experience Beginning

Class begins with the expectations gathered from all the other classes students and teachers have been in. In most classes all that is required, expected and honoured is the intellect. And so the student shows up ready to engage intellect. Heart, body, spirit, have had no place in the classroom.

If you desire something different—invite it, make space for it. Everyone is just waiting for: inspiration, movement, love, confidence, individuality to be invited in.

"All truth goes through three stages:
First it is ridiculed.
Then it is violently opposed.
Finally, it is accepted as self-evident."

~: *Arthur Schopenhauer* :~

Making Things into Process

Drums are about the heart. About mother and earth and our own rhythms. In drum making workshops I tell students that the class is not so much about making the drum as it is a process of making a drum. The drum you make you will use sometimes, but what you get from the process you may carry around all of the time. Making a drum is more about how you make it than having the drum at the end of the making.

We do a guided journey where students connect to their power animal, and the larger reason that at this time in their life they are making a drum. The drum comes to life with the awareness of what it means. This is the same for any class. It comes to life when it is connected to the life of the student-and the teacher. Power lives in each person's journey.

I go further in my drum making class. The model that I use, is the four directions: intellect, heart, body and spirit. For a five day drum making workshop I assign different elements to each day. Monday is about spirit... Tuesday; intellect... Wednesday heart... Thursday body... and Friday spirit again. We begin and end with spirit. Since learning is really about unlearning—we go backwards from east to north, to west, south and back to east.

When I add this theory to the week with some exercises to reflect on each days intent, it works. Reality accepts, and goes along with theory. I go further. I ask people to decide what direction they feel closest to - and then we talk about how that direction relates to each day, and the class in general. For example, this summer, the people with the direction of the west decided to bring a song to begin with on Wednesday, and a prayer to end with. Each group takes on the challenge of helping make their direction, their way of perceiving, more noticeable throughout the week... in whatever way they wish. It is important to allow room for peoples' inspiration, with as few expectations as possible.

Metaphor & Power

With only a word
you can make anything into anything else.

"*It is not a sign of good health to be well
adjusted to a sick society.*"
~: *J. Krishnamurti*

Only infinite patience
produces immediate results.

∼: *A Course in Miracles* :∼

As they become known and accepted to ourselves,
our feelings, and the honest exploration of them,
become sanctuaries and fortresses and spawning grounds
for the most radical and daring of ideas...

∼: *Audre Lorde* :∼

A Theme

Give them a theme,
a story, a reason
to go on the path you travel,
and then they will be drawn along
on a journey of discovery.

Explain the reasons
to go along the path,
and you shall excite them,
you shall inspire them,
and yourself, to live up
to the possibilities of the story.

The journey is only as exciting
as you can possibly make it—
or it is as boring as you let it be.

The heights, and the valleys
are all equally present.
You choose if you wish
to look out over the world,
or create a myth
in which to live, or both.

Knowing What to Keep

The book Silent Spring, written in 1962, which awakened the world to the dangers of DDT, which told the scientific story of DDT's bioaccumulation started with a story.

It opens, "There was once a town in the heart of America where all life seemed to live in harmony with its surroundings."

She led into the facts with a myth, a way to piece it all together. That is what a good teacher, leader, facilitator does—they give the framework to fit all the pieces together. That is the stuff of philosophy, religion, business and education. In our world so full of information, the important information is how to make sense of it all. Knowing what to keep and what to throw out. Story, myth and metaphor create meaning, out of the pieces.

Silence & Magic

The magic of a group happens in the emptiness.
Allow it, allow the inspiration that comes from nothing,
and the group will be able to live in magic.
The individuals will be present because they must be.

It is from the silence that the magic appears.

The more accepting of silence participants
are the more magic is possible.

Being Childlike

The separation of adult and child is the root of the confusion that is felt by those in the final stage of 'growing up' in our society. Adults can act like children, children can act like adults.

The simple difference is that adults usually have a certain amount of responsibility of a certain kind. Children have another type of responsibility as Tamalei says, "My work is play."

Well, my play is work. And so is yours—if you choose to see it that way—or you could choose to see it as tedious.

You choose, I choose—we all scream for ice cream!

Stories of Your Life

There is nothing more powerful
than the stories of your life.

They are stronger than your thoughts,
they hold your feelings, fears and beliefs,
and how you make your dreams real...
where you live.

Keep the stories that feed your soul.
They are sacred.

Share the ones which make you strong.
Let go of the ones which hurt and weaken you.

*Being true to yourself
is the one and only
Yurok Indian law.*

~: *Renee Locks* :~

Nothing!

"Take this onion" says the Zen master to his young disciple, "and peel away its layers."

The student holds the onion, looking at the brown skin. She slowly peels the skin off. Then the next layer—wondering what she will find in its middle—meticulously and mindfully she peels away layer after layer until, to her dismay, there is nothing in the centre. The last layer peels away like the first and then there is nothing.

The master, later in the day, sees the disciple sitting among the peels of the onion looking dismayed.

"What have you found in the centre of the onion?" asks the master.

"Nothing!" replies the student.

A grin spreads across the master's face. "The onion is no more, that is true, but if you raise your eyes from the place that the onion had been you will see that the whole world now rests in front of you. Nothing and everything are indeed very close to one another."

In all our lives
there is a time to cross
the imaginary line
from dependence to independence.

Making Time for Desire

Have you ever passed by something,
and said to yourself, 'I'll get to it later,'
then the later never happened?
Now is the only time.
You have a chance to do what you want to do.
You can't count on tomorrow.
Trust that your desire will bring you
where you have to go.
Let it draw you along. Let it lead you.

Trust it.
Begin now.

Be The Last Leader

Our role as true leaders is to ensure, that no one will have to do our job in the future. If we have taught people to learn, to think, to decide for themselves then they will no longer need our ideas, opinions etc. We can all move onto the next phase of being-in-the-world-playing with who I am.

I look forward to sitting on a little hill, singing my songs to the world-like birds have done forever. Letting my song go out to a world that listens with different types of ears; some who hear, some who notice a sound, others who dance, cry, or laugh. Most, however, will pass by on their own path, not noticing.

"The furthest
journey in one's life,
is from your head
to your heart."

Final Prayers

The last time I saw my "Bubbie"
(Yiddish for grandmother)
she offered three wishes,
and I offer them to you:

Take Care of Yourself

Good Luck

I Love You

*Say your prayers,
live your dreams, be kind.
Thanks for listening.*

Books, People, and Organizations to Inspire, Enlighten and Deepen your world.

Books

Shamanic Dream
by Anugama

Calling the Circle, the First and Future Culture
by Christina Baldwin

Coming to Our Senses
By Morris Berman

The Sacred Pipe: Black Elk's Account of the Seven Rites of the Oglala Sioux
by Joseph Epes Brown Ed

The Shamanic Way of the Bee: Ancient Wisdom and Healing Practices of the Bee Masters
by Simon Buxton and Ross Heaven

Sacred Drums (for the Shamanic Journey)
by Laura Chandler

The Spontaneous Fulfillment of Desire: Harnessing the Infinite Power of Coincidence
by Deepak Chopra

The Seven Spiritual Laws of Success: A Practical Guide to the Fulfillment of Your Dreams (based on Creating Affluence)
by Deepak Chopra

The Ecology of Imagination in Childhood
by Edith Cobb

The 7 Habits of Highly Effective People

by Stephen R. Covey
The 8th Habit: From Effectiveness to Greatness
by Stephen R. Covey

The Shamanic Drum: A Guide to Sacred Drumming
by Michael Drake

Drum Medicine
by David and Steve Gordon

Think and Grow Rich
by Napoleon Hill

Soul Retrieval: Mending the Fragmented Self Through Shamanic Practice
by Sandra Ingerman

The Fallacy of Wildlife Conservation
By John Livingston

In the Absence of the Sacred: The Failure of Technology and the Survival of the Indian Nations
by Jerry Mander

Shamanic Experience: A Practical Guide to Psychic Powers
by Kenneth Meadows

Shamanic Spirit: A Practical Guide to Personal Fulfillment
by Kenneth Meadows

Black Elk Speaks: Being the Life Story of a Holy Man of the Oglala Sioux
by John G. Neihardt

Awaken the Giant Within: How to Take Immediate Control of Your Mental, Emotional, Physical and Financial Destiny!
by Anthony Robbins

Shamanic Journey Drumming
by Evelyn Rysdyk & C. Allie Knowlton

The Fifth Discipline
by Peter M. Senge

Seven Arrows
by Hyemeyohsts Storm

The Psychology of Achievement: Develop the Top Achiever's Mindset
by Brian Tracy

Tao Te Ching
by Lao Tzu

The Changing Nature of Man
By J.H. Van Den Berg

The Aims of Education
by Alfred North Whitehead

Better Than Good: Creating a Life You Can't Wait to Live
by Zig Ziglar

Organizations

Anderson Consulting Group
www.andersonconsultinggroup.com 610.918.7461

Association for Humanistic Psychology
www.ahpweb.org   800.628.2783 or 703.683.8100

Babson College
www3.babson.edu 781.235.1200

Body Mind and Spirit
http://bodysoulspiritexpo.com 877.560.6830

California Institute of Integral Studies
www.ciis.edu 415.756.100

CBC Television
www.ottawa.cbc.ca 613.288.6491

CEO Group
www.ceo.co.nz 646.356.9025

Center for Creative Leadership
www.ccl.org/leadership/index.aspx 336.545.2810

Center for Meaningful Work
www.workwithmeaning.com 888.252.WORK (9675)

Institute of Cultural Affairs
www.icaworld.org 416.691.2316

Deloitte Consulting
www.deloitte.com 416.874.3874

Discovery Channel Body Mind and Soul
www.discovery.com

Ernst & Young
www.ey.com 888.865.4703

Fetzer Institute
www.fetzer.org 269.375.2000

Findhorn
www.findhorn.org +44.0.1309.690311

Franklin Covey
www.franklincovey.com 205.298.9050

Gestalt Institute
www.gestalt.on.ca 416.964.9464

Halliburton School of the Arts
www.haliburtonschoolofthearts.ca 866.353.6464

Holistic Junction: Media Positive Radio
www.holisticjunction.com/mediapositiveradio.cfm

Hollyhock
www.hollyhock.ca 800.933.6339

Innovation Network
www.innonet.org 202.728.0727

Institute of Noetic Science
www.noetic.org 707.775.3500

Naropa – Authentic Leadership
www.naropa.edu/leadership 303.444.0202

Of Spirit.com Healing Body Mind and Spirit
www.ofspirit.com/radio.htm 207.967.9892

Omega Institute for Holistic Studies
www.eomega.org 800.944.1001

Peak Potential
www.peakpotentials.com 604.983.3344

Pecos River Learning Center
www.pecosriver.com 800.622.2025 ext. 400

Peter Senge and the Learning Organization
www.infed.org/thinkers/senge.htm

Pricewaterhouse Coopers
www.pwcglobal.com 416.863.1133

Shamanicteachers.com
www.shamaniccircles.org

Soul Restore
www.soulrestore.com 800.491.7738

Spirit in business
www.spiritinbusiness.org

Spiritus Healing Center
www.spiritushealingcenter.com 604.982.0014

TranceDance
www.trancedance.com 512.708.888

WSRadio.com Total Wellness Radio
www.wsradio.com 858.623.0199 ext. 101

WNED Think Bright Lifelong Learning
www.thinkbright.wned.org 716.845.7000

Center for Visionary Leadership
www.visionarylead.org

VisionTV
www.visiontv.ca 416.368.3194

People

Les Brown
www.lesbrown.com 800.733.4226

Jack Canfield
www.jackcanfield.com 805.563.2935

Deepak Chopra
www.chopra.com 888.424.6772

Stephen Covey
www.stephencovey.com

Mark Victor Hansen
www.markvictorhansen.com 949.764.2640

Napoleon Hill
www.naphill.org 219.989.3166

Harvey Mackay
www.harveymackay.com 800.622.5299

Anthony Robbins and Associates
www.anthonyrobbinsdc.com 888.871.8909

Jim Rohn
www.jimrohn.com 800.929.0434 (in the U.S.) 817.442.5407

Brian Tracy
www.briantracy.com 858.481.2977

Denis Waitley
www.deniswaitley.com

Ziglar Training Systems, Inc.
www.zigziglar.com 800.527.0306

About the Author

David Aubrey Berger, M.E.S. lives in Toronto and spends, as much time as he can, playing with his children, family and friends. He is the executive director of the Living Education Institute, Co-founder of the Toronto Independent High School, as well as the director and co-creator of the annual Aleila Festival (of Expressive & Healing Arts). He also teaches drumming, and drum making at the Haliburton School of the Arts.. He lectures widely, and loves to work with groups, companies, schools, and individuals facilitating their potential.

At root all of the his work has one goal—to bring earth based wisdom, and the sense of our indigineity to people. This happens through interconnection, ceremony, celebration, personal reflection and meditation. It is a shamanic path that is personal and yet longs to be told and to be shared.

The Living Education Institute is a non-profit organization founded in the fall of 2000. It offers teacher training, personal development, and other courses and workshops to facilitate a culture of inspiration, potential and possibility.

David spent the first summer of life on a lake in the Canadian woods, and the great Canadian wilderness has been a significant factor in his thinking and being.

Thank you for taking the time to read this book. As appreciation I offer you the following opportunity:

Eco Leadership Workshop Coupon

This coupon entitles the bearer to attend a Level 1 Eco Leadership workshop **for free.** It may be used at any time and is transferable.
Visit my website at www.LivingUniversity.com
for dates and locations.

Notes & Thoughts

The Enemy Within